The Truth About Trump

You Decide

10% of Gross Profit to be donated to Red Cross!

Spencer S. Pierson

Please leave a review on Amazon.

Locomotive Ventures LLC

The Truth About Trump: You Decide

Spencer S. Pierson

Disclaimer: This book is not affiliated with Donald Trump or the Trump Family, nor is it affiliated with The Clintons or any other people or government agencies mentioned within this book. The intention of this book is to present the most unbiased facts available obtained mainly from "unbiased" government organizations. The author and the publisher intend readers to make their own conclusions on all parties mentioned within this book and assess the accuracy of the facts themselves. While every precaution has been taken in preparing this book, the author and the publisher assume no responsibility for errors or omissions. Neither is any liability assumed for damages resulting, or alleged to result, directly or indirectly from the use of information contained herein. If you do not wish to be bound by the above, you may return this book with receipt to the publisher for a full refund of the purchase price.

This book is available for bulk discounts. See contact above.

Library of Congress Control Number: 2020905260

Digital Edition ISBN-13: 978-1-7347822-0-2

Published By Locomotive Ventures LLC

DEDICATION

This book is dedicated to all of the small business owner's who are trying their best to survive in challenging state, local, and federal regulatory environments.

CONTENTS

ACKNOWLEDGMENTS

Thank you to my mom and dad (James and Lori Pierson-Herrera) for supporting me on my experiments with entrepreneurship, raising financing, investing, and teaching me business in execution. Also, a big thank you to my Dad for proof reading and editing this book. I would also like to thank any additional family, friends, colleagues, and anyone else who purchases my books.

1 TRUMP CHARACTERISTICS

With the 2020 Election just around the corner, the battle between the Republicans and the Democrats continue. The fact that our nation cannot work together on issues that both sides care about is extremely depressing: lowering medication prices, and infrastructure. It is time to assess the performance of Donald Trump, so that you can decide whether or not you want to reelect him. Let's start out by exploring who Donald Trump is and who he is not. What are the traits associated with Donald Trump?

All of the facts and data presented in this book will come from the most neutral sources I can think of: Federal Government Agencies, or straight from the horse's mouth backed up with additional data. In a few cases, I may have to resort to news articles for sources of data because I was unable to find anything else.

I hope this book will help you decide whether you want to re-elect Trump or not.

Grew the Fortune Started by his Dad:

Depending on whom you ask, the estimation of Donald's starting net worth varies wildly. In his book, The Art of the Deal, Donald Trump claims that he had a net worth of around $200,000 tied up in buildings by the time he graduated from Wharton. The decision of to believe that Donald Trump had a net worth of $200,000 out of college, borrowed $1 million from his dad to start his business, or borrowed millions from his father is entirely up to you. The highest inheritance number I have seen is $413 million. Regardless of the size of Trump's inheritance is the fact that he built buildings that became worth millions of dollars that were completely different from the buildings his dad built. As of this writing, Trump is worth $3.1 billion, a huge increase from his said inheritance and his said net worth out of college. Obviously Trump has been effective at growing his family fortune and not losing it.

Built Impressive Buildings:

There is no way anyone can deny that Donald Trump built impressive buildings. They can be found all over the World. Trump Tower, his most well known building; is known for a lobby of pink granite, bronze, and a waterfall.

Lives Well:

Donald Trump has the ideal lifestyle all of us want. He has the freedom (if he chooses) to do what he wants whenever he wants. He lives in his dream home inside of his own building and has fun toys to play with including: a private jet, a collection of cars; previously he had a yacht, and glamorous entertainment venues. He can go wherever he wants whenever he wants. Also, Donald Trump can stop working if he chooses. He is the symbol of the freedom everyone wants to achieve in the American Dream.

Is Charitable:

In addition to raising over $16 million through his foundation from 2001 to 2017, he also fixed New York City's Wollman Rink for cost. Of the money raised by the Donald J. Trump Foundation, Donald Trump or his businesses contributed approximately 23% of it. After hearing about a widow whose husband farmer committed suicide to keep the farm operating and in the family, Donald Trump threatened to sue the bank for murder and harassment to help save the farm. After working with prominent radio host Don Imus and businessman Frank Argenbright, the story went public, $100,000 was raised to pay the mortgage, and a mortgage burning ceremony was held in Trump Tower. As President of the United States, Donald Trump currently donates his $400,000 presidential salary to various charities or government agencies adding up to $1,600,000 in four years. If he is elected for another 4 years, another $1,600,000 will be donated. Do you think Donald Trump is charitable?

Is Affable to Common Folks:

Living in a town where Trump is a prominent figure, I have heard stories about how approachable he his. We live next to one of Trump's golf courses. My dad's friends have described Donald Trump as friendly and pointed out that he took fifteen minutes of his time to engage them and their wives in conversation. Would most celebrities or politicians give you that amount of time?

Is Patriotic:

Donald Trump has always had a giant flagpole with a

huge American flag on it at his golf course in the city of Rancho Palos Verdes, and he worked hard with the city and coastal commission to ensure that it could stay despite it being too tall for RPV's height restrictions.

Smart enough to lose his fortune and make it back:

In the 1990s Donald Trump lost his focus as a Real Estate Developer borrowing money that he should not have, guaranteeing debt that should not have been guaranteed, buying luxuries, and buying very different businesses from real estate. His splurges included a mega yacht, an airline, and three mega casinos. To top it all off, there was a recession and the real estate market was terrible. To turn his business and his life around Donald Trump became motivated and optimistic. He began to focus on new projects core to his business and divest businesses that were losing money, did not fit his portfolio, or that he did not have emotional attachment to. He also sold his mega yacht and his airline. He began to focus on the solution instead of the problem. He even negotiated a multi year deferment of interest payments. Today he is a billionaire yet again. Is this problem solving a seemingly impossible situation an important quality for a President? What do you think?

Has the Ability to Assess Key Strategic Issues:

In business school you learn to analyze key strategic issues. Having gone to The Wharton School of Finance and spent all of his life in business, Donald Trump definitely knows how to do this. Issues are usually analyzed through Porter's Five Forces. Let's do some analysis on the U.S. Economy prior to Donald Trump becoming President using Porter's Five Forces:

Competitive Rivalry	Supplier Power (World)	Buyer Power (U.S.)
• High • Countries Competing for: Jobs, money, energy resources, labor • Over 200,000 U.S. manufacturi ng jobs lost • At mercy to more expensive	• High • Manipulate currency • Legacy systems with Huawei • Foreign influence of politicians • Implement tariffs • 50% tariff on motorcycles	• Low • Partisan bickering holding back trade deals=gr eatest threat • Political power held by elite politician s catering to special

foreign oil • Higher labor rates than abroad • Competing against foreign higher skilled workers and low skilled illegal immigrants • Average world wide corporate tax rate of 22.5% compared to U.S. rate of 38.9% in 2016	being exported to India but 0% tariff on Indian motorcycles coming into U.S. • Ability to provide less expensive products • Corporate inversions for lower tax rates	interests (compani es that enjoy cheaper labor, lower taxes, and higher skilled work force in a foreign country)
Threat of Substitution	Threat of New Entry	
• High • Taiwan, Vietnam, China, Mexico, Africa, India, Illegal immigrants	• High • Lots of poor countries and competition for jobs	

Donald Trump's strategy was to improve the lives of all Americans by focusing on Jobs, Fair Trade, and controlling resources.

Has the Ability to Negotiate Deals that Work for Everyone:

In 1975 at age 29, Donald Trump began to negotiate the deal for his iconic Trump Tower. He was juggling a lot of balls at the time, but had yet to build anything. He was trying to build The Grand Hyatt and brand his location as the best location for a convention center. Donald tried to get the owner of the main site of Trump Tower to sell it to him. The owner did not bite no matter how appealing Trump made the deal. Donald stayed in touch. Three years went by since his first meeting with the owner of the future Trump property. The owner of the property started to experience financial issues, and a new CEO was put in charge. Recognizing Donald as the man who sent their company so many letters, the new CEO agreed to meet with him. After some difficulty following up with the new CEO, Trump was finally able to make a deal to buy the future site of Trump Tower and the underlying land lease for $25 million. Trump left the meeting with a signed letter of intent. To build the building that Trump envisioned, Trump had to acquire several other pieces of land and negotiate a lot of zoning changes with the city.

Other points of the Trump Tower deal:

1. Become 50, 50 partners with the owner of the underlying land to convince the bank to finance the project
2. Buy the air rights above Tiffany for $5 million
3. Extend the lease on the 4,000 square foot site next to Tiffany from 25 years to 100 years at a slightly increased rent in exchange for not exercising the option to buy, acquired from Tiffany
4. Keep his project a secret until all elements of the deal were assembled
5. Finalize and execute the contract for the main land of the future Trump Tower site despite the owner trying to back out of their letter of intent agreement.
6. Obtain 421-A Tax Abatement from New York
7. Negotiate zoning, building height, and building design with city planning and neighborhood and historical councils

The total Trump Tower project wound up costing around $190 million. At the time, according to The Art of the Deal, the building brought in $240 million in revenue and $10 million for Donald Trump acting as a sales agent. The retail space below Trump Tower also generated a lot more money. Obviously, every one of Donald Trump's partners benefited significantly from this deal.

Has Practical Experience:

As you can see form the sections above, Donald trump has had a lot of practical experience in dealing with governments, cutting through restrictive regulation, negotiating his way out of financial trouble, and negotiating business deals where everyone made money. He has endured a lot of restrictive regulatory challenges that businesses large and small face. Do you think all of this experience in business and dealing with government are good qualifications for someone taking a government position?

Not a Career Politician:

According to Senate.gov, approximately 50% of the 115th congress has been state or territorial legislatures. Since the 111th congress, the average length of service has varied between 10.3 years and 8.8 years for the House of Representatives. The Senate's length of service has varied between 13.4 years and 9.7 years. Keep in mind that the term of a

House Representative is 2 years and a Senate

Representative is 6 years. Here are some other statistics:

Occupation/ # of Members	**Representatives**	**Senate**
Public Service/Politics	194	44
Business	179	29
Law	168	50
Education	79	20
Total Members in Congress	435	100

According to data above, do you think most politicians are career politicians?

Another interesting statistic is the trust level of each of these occupations:

Occupation	% of People Who Believe These Professions Have Low Ethical and Honesty Standards
Real Estate Agents	19%
Building Contractors	20%
Lawyers	28%
Business Executives	32%
Members of Congress	58%

I think of Donald Trump as being a mix of a real estate agent, building contractor, and business executive; all of which are a lot more trust worthy than members of congress. In 2016 Trump campaigned mainly on trade, jobs, cutting taxes, energy, cutting regulation, and immigration.

Thought Provoking Questions:

1. If a large group of people did not believe that Trump had the qualifications to be President of the United States and that the issues he raised were important, would Donald Trump have won the Electoral College 304 to 227?
2. Who would you trust more, Donald Trump or Congress?

3. Who would you trust more to be a politician, a career politician or a successful businessman with a track record that was able to figure out how to bounce back from financial ruin?
4. What are your impressions of politicians (State, Local, and Federal) in general?

Willing to do what is right Despite Special Interest:

Many of Donald Trump's policies have been unpopular with the Republican, Democratic Parties, and our allies. For example, dragging out trade negotiations is not necessarily in the business community's (Big and Small) best interests, especially with tariffs, but it is in the best interest of the workers in the United States that have lost their manufacturing or service jobs to overseas laborers.

Another example of Trump acting in the best interest of the common man instead of our giant drug manufacturers is the fact that Trump recently tweeted "I will soon release a plan to allow Florida and other States to import prescription drugs that are much cheaper than what we have now. Hard working Americans don't deserve to pay such high prices for drugs that they need." With their major Research and Development costs, this type of policy is definitely not in the best interest of drug companies.

Cracking down on illegal immigration is also not in the business community's (Big and Small) best interest because it is decreasing the supply of labor, driving wages up. With a steady stream of illegal immigrants coming in, there is a constant stream of cheaper labor.

Do you think Donald Trump is acting more in the interest of the common man than the "Fat Cat" Donors?

Here is Data on Trump and Clinton 2016 Campaign Funding Sources:

	Trump	**Clinton**
Donations of $200 or Less	$126,664,225	$316,663,376
Donations of $200.01 or Above	$86,174,854	$312,026,772
Self Funded by Candidate	$66,141,714	$1,450,335
PAC	$144,814	$1,785,191
Party	$9,303	$20,039

Clinton had raised much more from the $200.01 or above group, PAC's, and the Party. Trump invested $66,141,714 of his own money into his campaign, much more than what Clinton contributed.

Who do you think is more likely to give in to special interests, Donald or Hillary?

Rough Around the Edges:

It is a fact that Donald Trump has a particular style in business and politics. He is very blunt and uses only simple language. Sometimes Donald says things in a way that it can be misconstrued. If you attack him, expect to be attacked back.

Do you see Donald trump as a bully or a fighter? Do you think Trump's style is effective?

Read on to make your decision.

2 POLITICAL ACHIEVEMENTS

Political Accomplishments

Taxes:

In addition to benefitting many areas of the economy, the tax reform has led to a savings of $2,000 per year for a typical family of four, according to Donald Trump's Speech at The Economic Club of New York.

Continue on next page.

Donald Trump succeeded in passing a huge Tax Reform Bill. Let's take a look at the changes:

Single Tax Rates 2017	**Single Tax Reform 2018**	**Married Tax Rates 2017**	**Married Tax Reform 2018**
10% $0	10% $0	10% $0	10% $0
15% $9,325	12% $9,525	15% $18,650	12% $19,050
25% $37,950	22% $38,700	25% $75,900	22% $77,400
28% $91,900	24% $82,500	28% $153,100	24% $165,000
33% $191,650	32% $157,500	33% $233,350	32% $315,000
35% $416,700	35% $200,000	35% $416,700	35% $400,000
39.6% $418,400	37% $500,000	39.6% $470,700	37% $600,000

In addition to lowering tax brackets by at least a few percentage points and adjusting each bracket's dollar amount, Trump also increased the standard deduction for married couples from $12,700 in 2017 to $24,000 in 2018. Single filers went from $6,350 to $12,000 in 2018. This is money that does not get taxed!

Other Accomplishments of Trump Tax Cuts:

1. Raises child tax credit to $2,000 per child
2. Estate Tax Exemption increased from $5.6 million to $11.2 million
3. Short Lived Capital Investments can be expensed instead of depreciated over time
4. Section 179 Deduction Cap doubled to $1 million
5. 20% Deduction for pass through income from sole proprietorships, LLC's, and S-Corporations

In anticipation for and as a result of Tax Reform the biggest companies in the United States announced and paid out bonuses to employees. Here is a list of some of the companies, their bonuses and other actions due to tax incentives:

Company	Bonus/U.S. Investment	Total Bonus/U.S. Investment
AFLAC	• Increase 401K match from 50% to 100% of first 4% of employee contribution • $500 one time contribution to every employee's 401K • Free Hospital and accident insurance products • Increase U.S. Investment by 250 million over 3-5 years	
Alaska Airlines	• $1,000 for 28,000 employees • $118 million in incentive	• $1,000*28,000= $28,000,000

	bonuses	
AT&T	• $1,000 in bonus to 200,000 U.S. Employees • Invest additional $1 billion in U.S. in 2018	• $1,000*200,000= $200,000,000
Disney	• One time $1,000 bonus for more than 125,000 employees	• $1,000*125,000= $125,000,000
JP Morgan	• Hire 4,000 employees • Open up 400 new Chase Branches • Increase minimum wage to $15 to $18/HR for 22,000 employees	
Apple	• Promised to contribute $350 Billion to the U.S. Economy over 5 years	
U.S.	• $1,000 for	• $1,000*60,000=

Bancorp	nearly 60,000 employees • Increase minimum wage to $15 per hour	$60,000,000

Do you think that the Trump Tax Reform has helped everyone and stimulated the economy?

Jobs:

Since Donald Trump took office, the unemployment rate has dropped from 4.7% to 3.6% and Donald's incentives have helped create almost 7,000,000 jobs. That is a decline in unemployment of 23.4% from January 2017 to October 2017. During the same period during Obama's first term, unemployment rose 6.4%. Under Obama's second term, unemployment declined 37.5%.

Other unemployment and Job statistics from the Bureau of Labor Statistics and Trump's recent (2019) Economic Speech:

Ethnicity	Unemployment Rate	Types of Jobs	Total Jobs Created Under Trump
African	• Declined from	All Jobs	• Created nearly 7

Americans	7.7% to 5.4% • 30% decline in unemployment rate		million jobs
Hispanics	• Declined from 5.5% to 4.1% • 25.4% decline in unemployment rate	Manufacturing/ Construction	• Created 1.2 million jobs
Asians	• Declined from 4.7% to 3.6% • Decline in unemployment rate of 23.4%	Energy/Oil	• Created 120,000 Jobs
16 to 19 Year Olds	• Declined from 14.7% to 12.3% • Decline in unemployment	Mining	• Created 25,000 jobs

	rate of 16%		
Men 20 Years and Over	• Declined from 4.3% to 3.2% • Decline in unemployment rate of 25.6%	Manufacturing	• Created over 600,000 Jobs
Women 20 Years and Over	• Declined from 4.4% to 3.2% • Decline in unemployment rate of 25.6%		

Under the Obama administration approximately 200,000 manufacturing jobs had been lost. According to the Census Bureau, the number of Americans in poverty dropped from about 40 million to 38.1 million in 2018.

Do you think Donald Trump's policies are helping to create jobs and lift people out of poverty?

GDP:

According to data presented by the Federal Reserve Bank of Saint Luis, since Trump took office in 2017 to quarter 2 of 2019, GDP has grown 12.169% or about 4.86% per year. During the same period during his first term, Obama saw GDP grow 7.6% and 9.95% in his second term. That is respectively 3.04% and 3.98% annually.

Do you think Donald Trump's economic policies are helping to increase the growth rate of GDP?

Immigration:

During his campaign Donald Trump promised to reform the immigration system, crack down on people over staying their visas, and crack down on illegal immigration for the best interest of United States Citizens and legal immigrants.

In his immigration policy speech Donald Trump said, "While there are many illegal immigrants in our country who are good people, many, many this does not change the fact that many illegal immigrants are lower skilled workers who are workers with less education who compete directly against vulnerable American workers."

Here are the facts on illegal immigration according

to whitehouse.gov:

- More than 977,000 illegals were apprehended or deemed inadmissible at our southern border in 2019. An increase of 88% from 2018.
- More than 851,000 illegals have been apprehended between ports of entry in 2019. An increase of 115%.
- 163 miles of border wall is being built with 450 miles expected to be completed by the end of next year
- Mexico has enhanced their border security efforts by deploying thousands of troops to the border
- Agreements have been reached to have migrants apply for asylum and wait for the status of their application in their home country

Donald Trump has also been successful in getting companies to hire U.S. Citizens over foreign workers with exceptions, read this statement from PwC:

“As of August 2018, we have decided that the firm will not be hiring entry level job seekers who are or will be subject to the H-1B lottery, except as set forth below.

Certain groups may make exceptions to the above policy. Entry level job seekers who will need to participate in the H-1B lottery may be considered for the following groups within PwC (please note PwC may revise these exceptions in its sole discretion at any time):"

As the supply of workers that are U.S. citizens get smaller and the economy continues to be robust, creating significant demand for more workers than supply, there will be a greater need to start bringing in foreign labor again.

As of June 2019, according to "Government Employment and Training Programs: Assessing Evidence of their Performance," there are 1.6 million more job openings than unemployed people.

What do you think about merit based immigration policies as a way to combat crime?

What do you think about immigration policies as an economic stimulus for struggling U.S. citizens?

Wage Growth:

According to the Bureau of Labor Statistics, wage

growths in all industries have increased from 2.2% in December 2016 (Just Before Trump took Office) to 2.7% in September 2019. That is an increase in the wage growth rate of 22.7%! Factors driving this include almost full employment with an unemployment rate of just 3.6% in 2019, new immigration policies, and the creation of almost 7,000,000 jobs. Donald Trump is preventing illegal immigration by enforcing our southern border. He also wants to reform the H1B Visa program to a merit-based program. Because of the uncertainty surrounding regulation of the H1B Visa Lottery and Trump's "hire American's first initiative," companies like the Big 4 Accounting Firms have stopped hiring entry-level workers requiring the H1B Visa Lottery as of August 2018. Wage goes up when labor supply is low and labor demand is high.

Even the New York Times ran a story on November 10th 2015 titled "Large Companies Game H1B Visa Program, Costing the U.S. Jobs."

From December 2016 to September 2019, the manufacturing job wage growth rate increased from 2.2% to 2.8%, and the construction wage growth rate increased from 1.9% to 3.5%.

Do you think Trump's pro business agenda and Trump's immigration policy is helping to drive wages up for Americans?

Trade:

Since taking office Trump has renegotiated the North American Free Trade Agreement (NAFTA) with Mexico and Canada. To gain access to cheaper labor, car companies have been moving car manufacturing to Mexico for years. As part of the new USMCA, according to United States Trade Representative website, to level the labor playing field for U.S. Citizens, 40-45% of automobile content must be made by workers earning $16 an hour. Helping small businesses out, Canada has raised import value from C$20 to C$40 (Canadian Dollars) to be exempt form taxes. Mexico will provide tax-free shipments for items up to a value of $117 dollars.

All of the environmentalists should also be somewhat satisfied with USMCA because USMCA enacts:

1. Subsidies are prohibited that encourage illegal, unreported, and unregulated fishing
2. Prohibition of shark finning, and commitment to work together to protect sea life (whales and sea turtles) and habitats
3. First ever guidelines to improve air quality, reduce and prevent marine litter, and provide

procedures for environmental impact assessments

Do you think these new rules will help protect United States' Jobs and promote fair treatment of workers in Mexico?

Now lets talk about China. According to the 2017 Report to Congress on China's WTO Compliance, "After its accession to the World Trade Organization (WTO) in 2001, China was supposed to revise hundreds of laws, regulations and other measures to bring them into conformity with its WTO obligations, as required by the terms set forth in its Protocol of Accession. U.S. policymakers hoped that the terms set forth in China's Protocol of Accession would dismantle existing state-led policies and practices that were incompatible with an international trading system expressly based on open, market-oriented policies and rooted in the principles of non-discrimination, market access, reciprocity, fairness, and transparency. But those hopes were disappointed."

Do you think it is fair that China joined our trade organization but refuses to play fair?

Again, China is another cheap alternative to labor in

the United States, costing the United States jobs. Cheap labor may be good for American companies, but it is not good for the overall U.S. economy.

To bring China to the negotiating table, Trump began instituting tariffs on Chinese goods coming into the United States. As of August 7th 2019, according to The Wall Street Journal, currently Trump has implemented **25%** import tariffs on **$250 billion** of Chinese goods.

How important do you think it is to have both free and fair trade?

Do you think Donald Trump is doing the right thing for jobs and the American economy?

Stock Market:

Since Donald Trump took office in January 2017, the Dow Jones has increased in value from 20,093.78 to 27875.62, an increase of 38.7%. After the Tax Cut was passed on December 22 2017, the Dow Jones jumped 7.69% from 24,719.22 to 26,616.71. The S&P 500, a more accurate measure of the broader market, increased 37%.

Over time the S&P 500 has had an average price to earnings ratio of 15.77 times earnings. The highest the S&P has been valued was at 123.73 times earnings, which was before the 2008 financial crisis. Currently the S&P is trading at 22.99 times earnings, suggesting that the market is hardly over valued and that there is a lot more room to run.

You can also consider the other metrics below:

	Price to Book Value	Price to Sales
S&P 500	• Maximum: 5.06 times book value • Average: 2.81 times book value • Minimum: 1.78 times book value • Current: 3.52 times book value	• Maximum: 2.20 times sales • Average: 1.54 times Sales • Minimum: .80 times sales • Current: 2.26 times Sales

Also, as of November 1st 2019 according to Fact Set, 76% of the S&P 500 companies reported earnings that beat analyst expectations and that 61% beat revenue expectations.

Which administration's policies do you think is responsible for the current stock market results?

Prison Reform:

Donald Trump worked with Congress to free up an additional labor source by signing the bipartisan First Step Act. According to firststepact.org, the First Step Act helps 200,000 people in federal prison rehabilitate, return from prison job ready, and provide major incentives for prisoners to get help so that they can succeed outside of prison.

Do you think former American prisoners should have priority for jobs over noncitizen immigrants?

Tackling the Opioid Epidemic:

According to whitehouse.gov, the Trump Administration has secured $6 billion over two years to fight opioid addiction. Also, high dose opioid prescriptions have fallen 16% between Trump's Inauguration and October of 2018. During that time, immigration and customs officials seized 2,300 pounds of fentanyl.

Emphasis on Upgrading Obsolete Workers:

According to "Government Employment and Training Programs: Assessing Evidence of their Performance," there are 47 employment and training programs spread across 15 Federal Government Agencies. In 2019, spending on these programs totaled 418.9 billion. The 2016 Presidential budget was the first to include continuous funding for grants to promote or expand apprenticeship programs. People who completed apprentice programs made an average of $240,037 more over their lifetime than those that didn't.

In response to the Trump Tax Cuts, many companies started paying for college or additional training for their employees. For example, Disney launched the Disney Aspire Program; which will pay 100% tuition for hourly employees to obtain additional training or receive a degree. Disney's program started with an investment of $150 million.

Worked with Companies to Gain Investment in the United States:

President Trump has also worked directly with companies to bring them to manufacture in the United States. Donald Trump actively recruited Foxconn and communicated his disapproval with the General Motors CEO when she threatened to shut down a car facility in the United States.

Increased Energy Independence:

What do you think the benefits are of not having to rely anyone else for energy production?

One of the big benefits of energy independence is for national security purposes. It also puts pricing power in our own hands instead of the hands of the Middle East or Russia. If supply outweighs demand, prices decrease. We are increasing energy supply. Increasing energy production in the United States also brings jobs home. Trump has already created 120,000 energy jobs.

Here is a look at the growth of production of each type of Energy according to the U.S. Energy Information Administration:

	2015 to 2016	2016 to 2017	2017 to 2018
Coal	Fell 18.27%	Rose 7%	Fell 2%
Natural Gas	Fell 2%	Rose 3%	Rose 12%
Crude Oil	Fell 6%	Rose 6%	Rose 17%
NGPL	Rose 4%	Rose 7%	Rose 14%
Nuclear	Rose 1%	Stayed Flat	Stayed Flat
Renewables	Rose 7%	Rose 8%	Rose 4%

As you can see, even renewable energy production is increasing under President Trump. All the "Greenies" out there should be happy about that.

Do you think pursuing energy independence and

increasing energy supply is a worthy cause for the President?

Invested in our Military:

How important do you think the U.S. Military is for our freedom? How much do you think is an appropriate spending amount? Which Countries do you think are the biggest threat to our freedom in the United States?

Currently, according to the Congressional Budget Office, Trump has requested that the defense budget be increased 2% to $718 billion. Of that $718 billion, $545 billion is designated for "normal, peacetime operations." Also, $173 billion is for emergencies and temporary war activities. The CBO estimates that the cost to implement the military's plans would increase 13% from 2024 to 2034.

Does this sound like a reasonable investment to you?

Ensured Countries in our Partnerships Paid their Fair Share:

According to history.state.gov, NATO was created to protect the United States, Canada, and Western Europe from the Soviet Union.

According to NATO, the countries that are members of NATO are supposed to contribute 2%

of GDP to Military Defense so that the United States only has to step into war when absolutely necessary. The only countries that have met or exceeded that guideline in 2014 (for Comparison purposes) have been The United States, Greece, and United Kingdom out of 28 member countries.

Who met the guideline in 2018? The countries that have increased their Military spending the most since Trump became president have been Latvia, Lithuania, and Romania. Lithuania increased its military spending from less than 1% of GDP to 2%. Latvia increased its defense spending from less than 1% of GDP to 2.03% of GDP in 2018. Romania increased defense spending from a little less than 1.5% in 2014 to 1.92% in 2018.

Overall, since Donald Trump became President, the majority of countries increased their military spending as a percentage of GDP despite still being in default. Only Croatia and Belgium decreased military spending in 2018. Also, Germany has been buying Russian oil and not contributing 2% to defend itself if Russia ever gets out of control. Donald Trump is getting these countries to contribute more money for their own defense.

Should the United States foot the bill to defend all of these countries if Russia ever gets out of control?

Do you think the NATO countries should contribute their fair share?

Should the United States be paying to defend Germany from Russia if Germany is buying resources from Russia?

Working to Lower Drug Prices:

According to the Food and Drug Administration, on December 18 2019, Donald Trump "issued a notice of proposed rulemaking that, if finalized would allow for the importation of certain drugs from Canada." This is the first step in lowering drug prices for the sick and making the greedy drug companies step back in line.

3 ACCUSATIONS

Racist:

Donald Trump has been accused of being a racist for the words he used during his speech to announce that he will be running for President of the United States.

However; according to New York Times Best Selling Author Ronald Kessler, in an article published by Chron, "When Donald opened his club in Palm Beach called Mar-a-Lago, he insisted on accepting Jews and blacks even though other clubs in Palm Beach to this day discriminate against blacks and Jews. The old guard in Palm Beach was outraged that Donald would accept blacks and Jews so that's the real Donald Trump that I know."

Trump got branded as a racist when he said, "When

Mexico sends its people they are not sending their best. They are sending people that have lots of problems and they are bringing those problems with them. They are bringing drugs, they are bringing crime, they are rapists, and some I assume are good people."

Did Donald Trump do the right thing by insisting that African Americans and Jewish people be allowed at Mar-A-Lago despite backlash? Or should he have allowed Palm Beach to continue business as usual?

Lets take a look at some other quotes by Donald Trump from his immigration policy speech.

"While there are many illegal immigrants in our country who are good people, many, many this does not change the fact that many illegal immigrants are lower skilled workers who are workers with less education who compete directly against vulnerable American workers."

"Hillary Clinton for instance, talks constantly about her fears that families will be separated; but, she is not talking about the American families who have been permanently separated from their loved ones because of a preventable homicide.

We will treat everyone living or residing in our

country with great dignity, so important, we will be fair, just, and compassionate to all. But our greatest compassion must be for our American citizens."

"On top of that she (Hillary) promises uncontrolled, low skilled immigration that continues to reduce jobs and wages for American workers and especially for African American and Hispanic workers within our country, our citizens."

"Zero tolerance for criminal aliens. At least 2,000,000 criminal aliens inside of our country."

Does Trump sound like a racist to you?

Or does he sound like someone that is protecting the interests of U.S. Citizens (including Legal immigrants) and National Security?

Should drugs and criminals be allowed to come across the southern border or should they be vetted?

Colluded with Russia to Steal the Election:

Donald Trump was accused of coordinating with Russia to influence the 2016 election. Despite believing that he was illegally spied upon and that the Dossier was a political hoax, Donald Trump allowed The Mueller investigation to finish.

Donald Trump was also accused of obstruction of

justice with regards to the Russia Investigation.

According to The American Bar Association, the Mueller Report found that Russia did interfere in the 2016 election but "did not find that the Trump Campaign, or anyone associated with it, conspired or coordinated with the Russian government in these efforts."

Also according to The American Bar Association in regards to obstruction of justice, the Mueller Report did not reach a conclusion as to whether or not Trump obstructed justice, but The Mueller report also stated, "While this report does not conclude that the President committed a crime, it also does not exonerate him."

Attorney General William Barr and Rod Rosenstein later "concluded that the evidence developed during the Special Counsel's investigation is not sufficient to establish that the President committed an obstruction-of-justice offense."

Do you think the Muller Investigation proves that Donald Trump committed a crime? Or does it prove that no crime was committed?

If Donald Trump allowed the Mueller Investigation to progress, do you think he obstructed justice?

Do you think that the Mueller Investigation went way beyond its scope (investigating if Trump colluded with Russia) and branched into Trump's private and business dealings?

Pressured Ukrainian President to Investigate Joe Biden:

The most recent accusation is that Trump withheld money from Ukraine in order to investigate Joe Biden and his son to keep Joe Biden out of the presidential race.

According to the second transcript of Donald's call with the Ukrainian Prime Minister, the first half of the call consisted of congratulations and discussing how the European Union does not do its fair share to help Ukraine out.

After discussing pleasantries and imbalanced relationship issues between the United States, Ukraine, and the European Union, the phone call turns to Donald Trump's investigation into the illegal spying of his campaign after The Mueller Report fails to incriminate him.

See excerpt below.

"I would like you to do us a favor though because our country has been through a lot and Ukraine knows a lot about it. I would like you to find out what happened with this whole situation with Ukraine, they say Crowdstrike ... I guess you have one of your wealthy people... The server, they say Ukraine has it. There are a lot of things that went on, the: whole situation … I think you are surrounding yourself with some of the same people. I would like to have the Attorney General call you or your people and I would like you to get to the bottom of it. As you saw yesterday, that whole nonsense ended with a very poor performance by a man named Robert Mueller, an incompetent performance, but they say a lot of it started with Ukraine. Whatever you can do, it's very important that you do it if that's possible."

The President of Ukraine goes on to assure Trump that they will help the United States get to the bottom of why his campaign was spied on without proper cause or procedure.

In response, President Trump goes on to introduce the lawyer that defended him in the Russia Investigation and talks about his displeasure with ambassadors from both countries. Joe Biden is not mentioned until the last part of this paragraph in the transcript.

"The former ambassador from the United States, the woman, was bad news and the people she was dealing with in the Ukraine were bad news so I just want to let you know that. The other thing, there's a lot of talk about Biden's son, that Biden stopped the prosecution and a lot of people want to find out about that so whatever you can do with the Attorney General would be great. Biden went around bragging that he stopped the prosecution so if you ·can look into it ... It sounds horrible to me."

The Ukrainian President goes on to talk about his new prosecutor and how the new prosecutor would be hired. He then says, " He or she (the prosecutor) will look into the situation, specifically to the company that you mentioned in this issue."

In the above quote, is the Ukrainian President talking about Crowdstrike (the company whose server may contain evidence of illegal spying on Trump's campaign) or the company that Biden's son worked for (not mentioned in the phone transcript)? You decide.

The transcript pretty much goes on to talk about the bad ambassadors and an unspecified prosecutor that was treated unfairly despite being a fair prosecutor. Trump tells the President that he will have the Attorney General call him and that "we will get to the bottom of it."

Again, is he talking about investigating Joe Biden or the investigation into illegal spying on his campaign?

Joe Biden is never mentioned again.

If you want, you can read the rest of the phone transcript to reach a conclusion on whether Donald Trump pressured Ukraine to investigate Joe Biden. The remainder of the transcript talks about Ukraine buying American oil, friends, visiting each other in Ukraine or the United States, and phone call wrap up.

Does it sound like Trump pressured Ukraine to investigate Biden to you?

What seems like the main purpose of the call: 1) Building a relationship 2) investigating illegal spying into the Trump campaign or 3) Investigating Joe Biden and his son?

Do you think this accusation is politically motivated?

Fraudster:

Donald Trump has been accused of tax fraud and using his charitable foundation for his own benefit. Lets take a look into the Donald J. Trump Foundation, The Eric Trump Foundation, and the Clinton Foundation.

A Note on Donald Trump's Taxes:

Despite being audited by the IRS every year, the Democrats believe that Donald Trump is committing tax fraud by paying zero to very little in federal income taxes.

The Democrats have tried for years to gain access to Donald Trump's tax returns.

Working in real estate I recently learned from a cost segregation specialist that "If you ever wondered how Donald Trump paid zero in Federal taxes, this is it."

What is cost segregation?

Cost Segregation is the allowance by the Federal Government to depreciate certain aspects of real estate much faster that the 27.5 year depreciation rate for residential real estate or 39 year depreciation rate for commercial real estate.

The Cost Segregation Specialist will take pictures of electrical panels, bushes, temporary walls, fixtures that would be left behind by a tenant, signage, flooring, appliances, and improvements that have been demolished. All of this property is then depreciated over 15, 7, or 5 years.

As a result, Trump or any other small real estate

owner who has significant construction expenses or incorrectly depreciated property in previous years either owes less in Federal Income Taxes or receives a refund.

In reality, Cost Segregation only defers income taxes (income taxes will eventually come due). If the business owner runs out of worthy projects or uses up all of their catch up depreciation, the result will be less quick depreciation and higher income resulting in higher income taxes. Also if the owner ever sells the real estate or business, all of the depreciation has to be recaptured and the owner will owe taxes on the depreciation.

That is how Donald Trump legally pays zero in Federal Income Taxes.

Donald J. Trump Foundation:

I have done my best to track down all tax returns for the Donald J. Trump Foundation. I was able to analyze the returns from 2001 to 2017. We are missing the tax return for 2007. In my analysis I found that Donald Trump had donated to his foundation from 2001 to 2008, 2015, and 2017. He personally donated approximately $3,870,770 (23% of total contributions) and raised approximately $12,634,745. Of that approximately $16,505,515, about $13,974,490 was given away. Donald Trump has claimed that his foundation has given $19 Million to charity, keeping in mind that I am missing information; my calculations can be used as a more conservative benchmark.

Between 2001 and 2017 the total expenses associated with the Donald J. Trump Foundation Equated to only 1% ($151,030 over 17 years) of the total amount given away (using my calculations).

The Trump Foundation has been accused of: 1) self dealing 2) illegally using the Foundation's fund raising capabilities to "raise Candidate Trump's profile days before the Iowa nominating caucuses by raising money for charity."

Donald Trump has been accused of using his foundation's money to buy 2 portraits of himself and a Tim Tebow helmet for a total of $42,000. One of the portraits was $20,000. What isn't being said, is that the portrait was bought at a charitable auction and benefited a nonprofit organization named Home Safe, an organization that protects "victims of child abuse and domestic violence" in Palm Beach, according to their website.

According to David Fahrenthold of the Washington Post, buying the painting and helmet using foundation money for a charitable cause may be illegal if the painting is on display in a Trump Golf Club or Hotel. According to David, the painting "is only allowed to be used for charitable purposes".

How are you supposed to use a painting for charitable purposes?

What money is Donald Trump making off of the portrait by hanging it in his Golf Club?

Was it not charitable that Melania Trump bought the painting at a charitable auction and increased her initial offer of $10,000 to $20,000?

Should the painting just be allowed to collect dust or should it be on display so that the artist gets recognized?

Do you think going after Trump for having his foundation buy a painting at a charity auction is petty?

Donald Trump has also been accused of "illegally using the foundation's fund raising capabilities to raise his campaign's profile before the Iowa nominating caucuses by raising money for charity."

According to the Des Moines Register, the fundraiser was held less than one week before the caucuses. At the time, Trump was fighting with Fox

News and refused to attend a debate Fox was hosting with all of Trump's adversaries. He instead held an event where he called for donations for various veteran charities. They raised approximately $5.6 million in donations and approximately 2.823 of that was collected by the Donald J. Trump Foundation and dispersed amongst many charities.

After the fundraiser, Donald Trump allowed his campaign staff to dole out the Donald J. Trump Foundation Funds in various amounts to various charities. During a series of rallies across Iowa, Donald Trump proceeded to pass out giant checks at the rallies to veteran charities; thus making him and his campaign look charitable while "illegally" increasing his political profile with Republican primary voters. Do you think that sounds inappropriate, or illegal?

Does the Clinton Foundation get to make any Clinton running for public office look permanently charitable?

Is it ever a bad time to raise money for U.S. veterans or soldiers?

Did the Clinton Foundation stop raising money when Hillary was campaigning or in public office?

The Eric Trump Foundation:

According to the Eric Trump Foundation Tax Returns, it has raised approximately $13 million between 2007 and 2017 and given away approximately $12.8 million. In 2007, the Eric Trump Foundation raised $318,702. The organization gave away $220,000 the same year with expenses of $74,358 (33.79% of money given away). The $74,358 is made up of $672 in administrative expenses and $73,686 of direct expenses.

It has been alleged that Donald Trump unjustly profited from the Eric Trump Foundation hosting its fundraiser at a Trump Golf Course, according to a Forbes article entitled "How Donald Trump Shifted Kids- Cancer Charity Money into his Business." Direct expenses went from $46,126 in 2010 to $322,370 in 2015. According to The Eric Trump Foundation Tax Return, only $79,904 went to Trump National Golf Club LLC in 2015. How can it be assumed that the entire $142,332 in 2011 and the entire $230,080 in 2013 went into Donald Trump's pockets, when there was no disclosure of such transactions? What about other expenses associated with the Charity Golf Event?

The amount of money raised by the Charity Golf event at the trump Golf course increased from $558,372 in 2010 to $1,201,459 in 2011 to

$2,282,370 in 2012. What about additional expenses incurred to Trump's Course due to an increase in scale of the Charity Golf Event?

Overall, keeping in mind that I am missing direct expense data for 2009, 2014, and 2016; The Eric Trump Foundation has spent approximately $1,047,678 in direct expenses and $439,283 on administrative expenses since 2007. Over 11 years, that is 11.54% of money given away.

After Donald Trump became President of the United States, Eric Trump issued the following Statement on his foundation's website:

"As Founder and President of this charity, it comes with great sadness to inform you that, effective December 31, 2016, I have decided to cease all direct fundraising efforts of my foundation. While I resigned with a heavy heart, it was a voluntary decision to enact these measures during the tenure of my father's presidency in order to avoid the appearance or assertion of any impropriety and/or a conflict of interest. Nonetheless, the foundation is being restructured and renamed, and under new leadership, it will continue its mission to support St. Jude Children's Research Hospital in the fight against pediatric cancer."

The Clinton Foundation:

I have been able to locate the 2017 Clinton Foundation Tax Return. According to the return, the Clinton foundation raised $70,776,528 in 2016 and $38,439,854 in 2017. In 2016 The Clinton Foundation only gave away $2,772,514 in grants. In 2017 The Clinton Foundation only paid out $2,420,380 in grants. Meanwhile, its expenses (salaries, fundraising fees, and other expenses) were $87,415,298 (2016) and $54,553,115 (2017). That means that The Clinton Foundation paid 3153% of the total amount given away toward expenses in 2016. 2254% of the amount given away went to pay expenses in 2017.

Chelsea Clinton has served on the Clinton Foundation Board of Directors since 2011. Hillary Clinton was Secretary of State under President Obama from 2009 to 2013.

The Clinton Foundation even paid $5,338,576 in rent. If the Clinton Foundation pays $5,338,576 in rent, do you think Donald Trump should be allowed to charge the Eric Trump Foundation fair market value for fundraiser services?

Here are some thought provoking questions.

Is it right to spend most of the money taken into a

charitable organization on operating expenses or should the majority of it be given away as grants?

Did The Clinton Foundation have to change its name (like the Eric Trump Foundation) and stop fundraising when Hillary Clinton was Secretary of State?

Did Chelsea Clinton and Bill Clinton have to (or volunteer) to resign from The Clinton Foundation's Board of Directors when Hillary Clinton was Secretary of State like Eric Trump to avoid appearance of a conflict of interest?

Did The Clinton Foundation have to stop fundraising when Hilary Clinton was campaigning as the Democratic Nominee, like Donald Trump was charged for illegally raising money for veterans as he campaigned as the Republican Nominee?

What do you think about Donald Trump and the Donald J. Trump Foundation and Eric Trump Foundation?

What do you think about Hillary Clinton and the Clinton Foundation?

Bully and Fascist:

Donald Trump has been accused of being a bully and a Fascist.

Donald Trump does come up with "nicknames" for all of his opponents and has a particular style that can be misconstrued and be rough. He comes up with names like Lyin Ted, Nervous Nancy, and Mini Mike. If someone attacks Donald Trump, he usually attacks him or her back. You can decide whether or not you think Trump's style is effective based on the information above.

Let's take a look at how Trump's opponents behave.

Milo Yiannopolis (a Conservative Commentator) was going to give a speech at UC Berkley and protestors greeted him by throwing bricks, breaking windows, starting fires, and tearing down barricades. As a result, his speech had to be cancelled.

Barron Trump, Donald Trump's son; has been called autistic and promoted as "this country's first homeschool shooter" by opponents of Donald Trump.

Tomi Lahren, a 25-year-old Conservative Commentator, had water thrown on her when she was out to a meal with her parents.

Kristjen Nielsen, the former Department of Homeland Security Secretary under President Trump was heckled while eating at a Mexican restaurant because of her views of the situation on the border of Mexico. Protestors yell, "How dare you spend your evening here eating dinner…Abolish ICE" and "Shame! Shame! Shame! Shame! Shame! Shame! Shame!"

Who do you think is a bully or fascist? Donald Trump? His opponents? Or both?

Would you consider Donald Trump more of a bully, a fighter, or both?

Should someone be shamed or bullied because they have a different point of view or way of thinking than others?

Based on your opinion and experience, have the Democrats made considerable effort to attempt to work with Donald Trump on issues that both sides care about (infrastructure, lowering drug prices)? Vice Versa?

Hates Women:

Donald Trump has been accused of hating women.

According to The Art of The Deal, in the 1980's Donald Trump put the first woman in charge of overseeing construction of a skyscraper in New York. Her name is Barbara Res. In his own words Donald Trump said "My own mother was a housewife all of her life. And yet it's turned out that

I have hired a lot of women for top jobs, and they've been among my best people. Often, in fact, they are far more effective than the men around them."

Here is a list of women that have been at the top of The Trump Organization.

1. Barbara Res- Donald's personal representative overseeing construction of Trump Tower and first women to be in charge of building a skyscraper in New York
2. Louise Sunshine- An Executive Vice President for 10 years at The Trump Organization
3. Blanche Sprague- Executive Vice President of Sales and Supervisor of Interior Design
4. Norma Foerderer- Donald Trump's Executive Assistant

4 CONCLUSION

In Conclusion:

I want you to make your own decisions about Trump and will only tell you briefly what I think. I hope you have felt that this book has been fair and neutral in its sources and truthful with its facts.

Love him or hate him, based on his economic performance, I think that Donald Trump has done a lot more good than harm. As Daymond John says, "Entrepreneurship is the ultimate equalizer." As economics improve and more people work in jobs, they will be forced to work together and to put all of their prejudices aside. More businesses will be started and more businesses will thrive.

I also think that it will be vary difficult to prove that Donald Trump pressured Ukraine to investigate Joe Biden based on both phone calls. It seems to me that Donald Trump's inquires were related to the investigation into whether or not his campaign was illegally spied on.

It would be a shame if everything reverted to business as usual in the United States Federal Government. Both Republicans and Democrats have made very poor decisions that have harmed this country. In business it is a priority to resolve disputes so that things can be accomplished. In politics it seems like creating disputes is priority so that nothing gets accomplished and power is maintained.

You environmentalists and marijuana lovers can't hate Trump too much. He thinks marijuana should be legalized for medical purposes and states should be able to make the choice to legalize it for recreational use. Also, Donald Trump has included environmental protections in his new trade agreement with Mexico and Canada.

Update During Financial Crisis:

In investing, when you diversify across countries, the idea is that if one country's markets go bad, the markets in other countries would be doing well enough to minimize any of your financial losses. Due to the nature of globalization and concentration of manufacturing within only one region, most supply chains in markets around the world are being disrupted with negative financial consequences. Additionally, the Financial Crisis is being spread to many countries around the world. Supply ships and cruise ships are not being allowed to enter U.S. ports.

Do you think Trump can be blamed for this economic crisis if many other countries are experiencing the same side effects? Emerging markets (SCHE) are down 32.4%, U.S markets (SCHX) are down 32.6%, and foreign markets (SCHF) are down 33.4%. Have politicians of every country pretty much built their countries on a financial house of cards?

Should countries around the world own most of their own means to production so that supply chains of their companies (employers) minimize interruption?

Does this situation make Trump's foreign and immigration policy more appealing (especially his dealings with Foreign Governments)?

Does this help make a case to bring manufacturing back to the United States (especially for: medication, medical equipment, telecommunication infrastructure, microchips, computers, and other necessary items)?

Businesses are shutting down around the world.

Hopefully this crisis will unite Democrats, Republicans, and Trump; thus driving our politicians to make better choices for our country.

Let us know what you think. To be continued…

5 BIBLIOGRAPHY

King, Larry, and Donald Trump, actor. *Trump in 1999: Oprah would be my VP choice.* Narrated by Larry King and Donald Trump, CNN, 1999, www.youtube.com/watch?v=bc90K7Kieek.

Trump, Donald, actor. *Donald Trump Weighs in on Marijuana, Hil.* Narrated by Donald Trump, GQ, 2015, www.youtube.com/watch?v=LqofXgLAI04.

Jaeger, Kyle. "President Trump Reiterates His Administration Will Let States Legalize Marijuana." *Marajuana Moment*, 30 Aug. 2019, www.marijuanamoment.net/president-trump-reiterates-his-administration-will-let-states-legalize-marijuana/.

"Paris Agreement." *unfccc.int*, United Nations, 2015, unfccc.int/sites/default/files/english_paris_agreement.pdf.

"Defence Expediture of NATO Countries (2011-2018)." *Nato.int*, NATO, 14 Mar. 2019, www.nato.int/nato_static_fl2014/assets/pdf/pdf_2019_03/190314-pr2018-34-eng.pdf.

"The north Atlantic Treaty." *North Atlantic Treaty Organization*, NATO, 4 Apr. 1994, www.nato.int/cps/en/natolive/official_texts_17120.htm.

"Civilian Unemployment Rate." *U.S. Bureau of Labor Statistics*, U.S. Bureau of Labor Statistics, www.bls.gov/charts/employment-situation/civilian-unemployment- rate.htm.

"U.S. Economy at a Glance." *Bureau of Economic Analysis*, U.S. Bureau of Economic Analysis, Oct. 2019, www.bea.gov/news/glance.

"Gross Domestic Product." *Federal Reserve of Saint Luis*, FRED, 2019, fred.stlouisfed.org/series/GDP.

Schouten, Fredreka. "Here's how much of his own money Trump spent on his campaign." *USA Today*, USA Today, 8 Dec. 2016, www.usatoday.com/story/news/politics/onpolitics/2016/12/08/donald-trumps-campaign-investment-hit-66-million/95178392/.

Carroll, Lauren. "Is Donald Trump self-funding his campaign? Sort of." *Politifact*, Politifact, 10 Feb. 2016, www.politifact.com/truth-o-meter/statements/2016/feb/10/donald-trump/donald-trump-self-funding-his-campaign-sort/ .

U.S. Bureau of Labor Statistics, U.S. Bureau of Labor Statistics, 7 Nov. 2019, www.bls.gov/opub/ted/2019/private-industry-compensation-costs-up-2-point-7-percent-from-september-2018-to-september-2019.htm .

Social Security Administration, Social Security Administration, www.ssa.gov/oact/cola/central.html . Accessed 21 Dec. 2019.

Wall Street Journal, Wall Street Journal, 20 Dec. 2019, www.wsj.com/market-data/stocks/peyields .

Gleeson, Patrick. *Zacks*, edited by Ryan Cockerham, Zacks, 31 Mar. 2019, finance.zacks.com/longterm- average-pe-dow-jones-3619.html.

multpl.com, multpl.com, 20 Dec. 2019, www.multpl.com/s-p-500-pe-ratio.

Butters, John. *FactSet*, FactSet, 1 Nov. 2019, www.factset.com/hubfs/Resources%20Section/Research%20Desk/Earnings%20Insight/EarningsInsight_110119.pdf.

Brookings, Brookings, 19 Dec. 2019, www.brookings.edu/interactives/tracking-deregulation-in-the-trump- era/.

Forbes, Forbes, 22 Dec. 2019, www.forbes.com/profile/donald-trump/#6d8d528247bd.

Ladika, Matthew, and David Fahrenthold, actor. *6-Foot Portrait Of Donald Trump Raises Q.* Narrated by Hallie Jackson, Today, 2016, www.youtube.com/watch?v=_FFWqcKcRao.

HomeSafe, HomeSafe, www.helphomesafe.org/about-us/.

Choma, Russ. "Donald Trump Ordered to Pay $2 Million for Charity Fraud." *Mother Jones*, 7 Nov. 2019, www.motherjones.com/politics/2019/11/donald-trump-ordered-to-pay-2-million-for-charity-fraud/.

Trump, Eric F. *The Eric Trump Foundation*, The Eric Trump Foundation, Dec. 2016, www.erictrumpfoundation.com/. Accessed 28 Dec. 2019.

Alexander, Dan. "How Donald Trump Shifted Kids-Cancer Charity Money Into His Business ." *Forbes.com*, Forbes, 29 June 2017, www.forbes.com/sites/danalexander/2017/06/06/how-donald- trump-shifted-kids-cancer-charity-money-into-his-business/#7952faa06b4a.

LLP, Mazars. "Return of Private Foundation 2017 The Donald J. Trump Foundation." *documentcloud.org*, Document Cloud, 14 Nov. 2018, www.documentcloud.org/documents/5280593-Trump-Foundation-2017-990.html.

"Various Tax Returns for The Donald J. Trump Foundation." *foundationcenter.org*, 990finder.foundationcenter.org, 990finder.foundationcenter.org/990results.aspx?990_type=&fn=trump+foundation&st=NY&zp=&ei=&fy=&action=Find.

"Various Tax Returns for The Eric F. Trump Foundation." *foundationcenter.org*, 990finder.foundationcenter.org, 990finder.foundationcenter.org/990results.aspx?990_type=&fn=trump+foundation&st=NY&zp=&ei=&fy=&action=Find.

"NY Suit Against Trump Foundation Explained." *You Tube*, AP Archive, 19 June 2018, www.youtube.com/watch?v=lVJkJrlR7bg.

"Donald Trump Veterans donations full press conference." *You Tube*, CNN, 31 May 2016, www.youtube.com/watch?v=eJ5kNEL0KzI.

"Various Eric F. Trump Foundation/Curetivity Foundation Tax Returns." *projects.propublica.org*, ProPublica, projects.propublica.org/nonprofits/organizations/208669454. Accessed 29 Dec. 2019.

Pfannenstiel, Brianne. "Des Moines fundraiser at center of New York lawsuit against Donald Trump, his foundation." *Des Moines Register*, Des Moines Register, 14 June 2018, www.desmoinesregister.com/story/news/2018/06/14/donald-trump-foundation-iowa-caucus-illegal-conduct-lawsuit/701564002/.

"Various Donald J. Trump Foundation Tax Returns." *projects.propublica.org*, ProPublica, projects.propublica.org/nonprofits/organizations/133404773. Accessed 29 Dec. 2019.

"Revenues in 2017: An Infographic." *Congressional Budget Office*, Congressional Budget Office, 5 Mar. 2018, www.cbo.gov/publication/53627.

"The Federal Budget in 2018: An Infographic ." *Congressional Budget Office*, Congressional Budget Office, 18 June 2019, www.cbo.gov/publication/55342.

Barragan, Bianca. "Donald Trump Allowed to Keep Illegally Huge Flagpole in RPV." *Curbed Los Angeles*, Curbed Los Angeles, 10 July 2014, la.curbed.com/2014/7/10/10077024/donald-trump-sort-of-wins-fight-for- 70foot-flagpole-on-his-rpv-golf.

"Crude oil prices started 2015 relatively low, ended the year lower."

U.S. Energy Information Administration, U.S. Energy Information Administration, 6 Jan. 2016, www.eia.gov/todayinenergy/detail.php?id=24432.

"Crude oil prices end the year lower than they began the year." *U.S. Energy Information Administration*, U.S. Energy Information Administration, 3 Jan. 2019, www.eia.gov/todayinenergy/detail.php?id=37852.

Manning, Jennifer E. "Membership of the 115th Congress: A Profile." *Congressional Research Service*, senate.gov, 20 Dec. 2018, www.senate.gov/CRSpubs/b8f6293e-c235-40fd-b895-6474d0f8e809.pdf.

McCarthy, Niall. "America's Most & Least Trusted Professions [Infographic] ." *Forbes*, Forbes, 11 Jan. 2019, www.forbes.com/sites/niallmccarthy/2019/01/11/americas-most-least-trusted-professions-infographic/#3d7bb607e94e.

"The Electorial College." *National Archives*, National Archives, www.archives.gov/electoral-college.

"Comparison of U.S.and International Prices for Top Medicare Part B Drugsby Total Expenditures." *hhs.gov*, hhs.gov, 25 Oct. 2019, aspe.hhs.gov/system/files/pdf/259996/ComparisonUSInternationalPricesTopSpendingPartBDrugs.pdf.

"2020 Presidential Campaign Finance." *Federal Election Commission*, FEC.gov, classic.fec.gov/disclosurep/pnational.do. Accessed 1 Jan. 2020.

"2020 Presidential Campaign Finance." *Federal Election Commission*, FEC.gov, classic.fec.gov/disclosurep/pnational.do. Accessed 1 Jan. 2020.

Amadeo, Kimberly. "US Federal Government Tax Revenue ." *The Balance*, thebalance.com, 21 Dec. 2019, www.thebalance.com/current-u-s-federal-government-tax-revenue-3305762.

"Revenues in 2016: An Infographic." *Congrssional Budget Office*, Congressional Budget Office, 8 Feb. 2017, www.cbo.gov/publication/52411.

"A Painful Pill to Swallow: U.S. vs. International Prescription Drug Prices." *waysandmeans.house.gov*, Prepared by Ways and Means Committee Staff, Sept. 2019, waysandmeans.house.gov/sites/democrats.waysandmeans.house.gov/files/documents/U.S.%20vs.%20International%20Prescription%20Drug%20Prices_0.pdf.

Katzeff, Paul. "How The New Trump Tax Brackets Impact Your Tax Rate ." *Investor's Business Daily*, Investor's Business Daily, 28 Mar. 2019, www.calvin.edu/library/knightcite/index.php.

Floyd, David. "Explaining the Trump Tax Reform Plan ." *Investopedia*, Investopedia, 2 Aug. 2019, www.investopedia.com/taxes/trumps-tax-reform-plan-explained/.

Shell, Adam. "List of companies that paid bonuses or boosted pay since tax bill passed." *USA Today*, USA Today, 25 Jan. 2018, www.usatoday.com/story/money/2018/01/11/list-companies-paid-bonuses-boosted-pay-since-tax-bill-passed/1023848001/.

Wells, Nick, et al. "These companies are paying bonuses with their tax savings." *CNBC*, CNBC, 26 Jan. 2018, www.cnbc.com/2018/01/26/us-companies-that- have-announced-bonuses-investments-after-tax-cut.html .

Haselton, Todd, and Lauren Feiner. "Apple's cash hoard now at $225.4 billion." *CNBC*, CNBC, 30 Apr. 2019, www.cnbc.com/2019/04/30/apple-now-has-225-billion-cash-on-hand.html .

Trump, Donald J., actor. *AMERICAN STRENGTH: President Trump Touts.* , Fox 10 Phoenix, 2019, www.youtube.com/watch?v=tXa1tk6vB6U.

"Number in Poverty and Poverty Rate: 1959 to 2018." *U.S. Census Bureau*, U.S. Census Bureau, 2019, www.census.gov/content/dam/Census/library/visualizations/2019/demo/p60-266/Figure7.pdf .

Semega, Jessica, et al. "Income and Poverty in the United States: 2018." *U.S. Census Bureau* , U.S. Census Bureau , 10 Sept. 2019, www.census.gov/library/publications/2019/demo/p60-266.html.

U.S. Department of Homeland Security, U.S. Customs and Border Protection, 9 Dec. 2019, www.cbp.gov/newsroom/stats/sw-border-migration .

"PwC Entry Level Visa Sponsorship Eligibility." *pwc.com*, PwC, 2018, www.pwc.com/us/en/careers/entry-level/eligibility.html

"North Atlantic Treaty Organization (NATO), 1949." *Office of the Historian*, Department of State United States of America, history.state.gov/milestones/1945-1952/nato 6 Jan 2020.

"About." *firststepact.org*, firststepact.org, 6 Jan. 2020, www.firststepact.org/about.

"U.S. primary energy consumption by energy source, 2018." *U.S. Energy Information Administration*, U.S. Energy Information Administration, 28 Aug. 2019, www.eia.gov/energyexplained/us-energy-facts/ .

"Why Energy Independence." *CarbonCycle Energy*, CarbonCycle Energy, 7 Jan. 2020, www.c2-energy.com/what-we-do/who-benefits/energy-independence/.

"Long-Term Implications of the 2020 Future Years Defense Program." *CONGRESS OF THE UNITED STATESCONGRESSIONAL BUDGET OFFICE*, CONGRESS OF THE UNITED STATESCONGRESSIONAL BUDGET OFFICE, Aug. 2019, www.cbo.gov/system/files/2019-08/55500-CBO-2020-FYDP_0.pdf .

"UNITED STATES–MEXICO–CANADA TRADE FACT SHEET Modernizing NAFTA into a 21st Century Trade Agreement." *Office of the United States Trade Representative*, Office of the United States Trade Representative, 7 Jan. 2020, ustr.gov/trade-agreements/free-trade-agreements/united-states-mexico-canada-agreement/fact-sheets/modernizing .

"2017 Report to CongressOn China's WTO Compliance." *2017 Report to CongressOn China's WTO ComplianceUnited States Trade Representative*, 2017 Report to CongressOn China's WTO ComplianceUnited States Trade Representative, Jan. 2018, ustr.gov/sites/default/files/files/Press/Reports/China%202017%20WTO%20Report.pdf.

"Ending America's Opioid Crisis." *whitehouse.gov*, whitehouse.gov, 7 Jan. 2020, www.whitehouse.gov/opioids/.

The Eric Trump Foundation, The Eric Trump Foundation, 2016, www.erictrumpfoundation.com/.

Trump, Donald J. "STATEMENT FROM PRESIDENT DONALD J. TRUMP." *Twitter*, Twitter, 7 Jan. 2020, twitter.com/realDonaldTrump/status/1192594646691729408/photo/1.

Martin, Allen, et al. "Live Report: Riot At Scheduled Milo Yiannopoulos Event At UC Berkeley." *You Tube*, KPIX CBS SF Bay Area, 1 Feb. 2017, www.youtube.com/watch?v=XImz4b2KtAw.

Riots Stop Milo Yiannopoulos Event At Be. , Wochit News, 2017, www.youtube.com/watch?v=TjaGWGPZPV4.

Fernando, Gavin. "Criticise Donald Trump all you want, but children are off-limits." *news.com.au*, news.com.au, 24 Jan. 2017, www.news.com.au/lifestyle/parenting/kids/criticise-donald-trump-all-you- want-but-children-are-offlimits/news-story/2543602d324faa218da3863f3f71a6d5.

Sblendorio, Peter. "Tomi Lahren 'embarrassed' after woman throws drink at her at Minneapolis restaurant ." *New York Daily News*, New York Daily News, 23 May 2018, www.nydailynews.com/news/politics/tomi-lahren-embarrassed-woman-throws-drink-article-1.4005099.

Lahren, Tomi, actor. *Conservative Heifer, Tomi Lahren gets WA.* , mrduckbears33, 2018, www.youtube.com/watch?v=kAgPY-fdWpE.

Nielsen, Kirstjen, actor. *Protesters disrupt DHS Secretary Kirstjen Nielsen at Mexican Restaraunt.* , CBS News, 2018, www.youtube.com/watch?v=RXVxpRq0e2U.

Trump, Donald J., actor. *Donald Trump Presidential Campaign Announcement Full Speech.* , C-Span, 2015, www.youtube.com/watch?v=apjNfkysjbM.

Trump, Donald J., actor. *Trump FULL Immigration Speech in Phoenix.* , ABC News, 2016, www.youtube.com/watch?v=lj-XOJsHKsE.

Romano, Robert. "Trump insisted on including Jews, blacks at Palm Beach golf course in 1990s." *Chron*, Chron, 4 Mar. 2016, www.chron.com/neighborhood/katy/opinion/article/Trump-insisted-on-including-Jews-blacks-at-Palm-9702222.php.

"President Donald J. Trump's Efforts to Combat the Crisis at Our Southern Border Are Delivering Results." *whitehouse.gov*, whitehouse.gov, 8 Oct. 2019, www.whitehouse.gov/briefings-statements/president-donald-j-trumps-efforts-combat-crisis-southern-border-delivering-results/.

"The Council of Economic AdvisGovernment Employment and Training Programs:Assessing the Evidence on their Performance." *whitehouse.gov*, whitehouse.gov, June 2019, www.whitehouse.gov/wp-content/uploads/2019/06/Government-Employment-and-Training-Programs.pdf.

"Telephone Conversation with PresidentZelenskyy of Ukraine ." *whitehouse.gov*, whitehouse.gov, 24 Sept. 2019, www.whitehouse.gov/wp-content/uploads/2019/09/Unclassified09.2019.pdf.

"Mueller finds no collusion with Russia, leaves obstruction question open." *American Bar Association*, American Bar Association, 11 Jan. 2019, www.americanbar.org/news/abanews/aba-news-archives/2019/03/mueller-concludes-investigation/.

Hotakainen, Rob. " Donald Trump and marijuana: Will the two biggest winners of 2016 get along? ." *McClatchy DC*, McClatchy DC, 9 Nov. 2016, www.mcclatchydc.com/news/politics-government/election/article113726634.html.

Trump, Donald J., actor. *Trump speaks at the Economic Club of New.* , CBS, 2019, www.youtube.com/watch?v=uYmTMNGe-Ww.

"Cost Segregation Services." *MossAdams*, MossAdams, 11 Jan. 2020, www.mossadams.com/services/accounting/tax/credits-and-incentives/tangible-asset-incentives/cost-segregation.

Pomerleau, Kyle, and Emily Potosky. "Corporate Income Tax Rates around the World, 2016." *taxfoundation.org*, Tax Foundation,

18 Aug. 2016, taxfoundation.org/corporate-income-tax-rates-around-world-2016/.

"Overview of PRC Taxation System." *PwC China*, PwC China, www.pwccn.com/en/services/tax/accounting-and-payroll/overview-of-prc- taxation-system.html. Accessed 17 Jan. 2020.

"50% import tariff on Harley Davidson unacceptable, India should remove it: Trump." *Live Mint*, Live Mint, 11 June 2019, www.livemint.com/.

"Trump Administration takes historic steps to lower U.S. prescription drug prices." *U.S. Food and Drug Administration*, U.S. Food and Drug Administration, 18 Dec. 2019, www.fda.gov/news-events/press-announcements/trump-administration-takes-historic-steps-lower-us-prescription-drug-prices.

"The 20 countries with the highest unemployment rate in 2017 ." *Statista*, Statista, 2019, www.statista.com/statistics/264656/countries-with-the-highest-unemployment-rate/. Accessed 24 Jan. 2020.

"Unemployment holds steady for much of 2016 but edges down in the fourth quarter." *U.S. Bureau of Labor Statistics*, U.S. Bureau of Labor Statistics, Mar. 2017, www.bls.gov/opub/mlr/2017/article/unemployment-holds-steady-for-much-of-2016-but-edges-down-in-fourth-quarter.htm.

https://www.latimes.com/business/story/2019-08-29/latest-round-of-trumps-tariffs-on-china-take-effect-on-many-consumer-goods

https://www.washingtonpost.com/sports/2018/12/19/trump-will-have-give-up-his-signed-tim-tebow-helmet-part-settlement/

Zumbrun, Josh. "U.S. Collected $63 Billion in Tariffs Through June ." *Wall Street Journal*, Wall Street Journal, 7 Aug. 2019, www.wsj.com/articles/u-s-collects-63-billion-in-chinese-tariffs-through-june-11565168400.

"S&P 500 Price to Book Value." *multpl.com*, multpl.com, 25 Feb. 2020, www.multpl.com/s-p-500-price-to-book.

"S&P 500 Price to Sales Ratio." *multpl.com*, multpl.com, 25 Feb. 2020, www.multpl.com/s-p-500-price-to-sales.

"Inflation Adjusted S&P 500." *multpl.com*, multpl.com, 25 Feb. 2020, www.multpl.com/inflation-adjusted-s-p-500.

"S&P 500 Earnings Yield." *multpl.com*, multpl.com, 25 Feb. 2020,www.multpl.com/s-p-500-earnings-yield.

ABOUT THE AUTHOR

Spencer Pierson is an author that is interested in politics because of the massive impact it has on the well being of all people and businesses within the United States. As an employee for a small real estate company, Spencer is aware of the challenges and impact that both federal and local policy have on small family offices. Spencer is extremely proud of his entrepreneurial heritage and looks forward to sharing his experiences with the less fortunate so that they can one day be personally and financially successful. If there is one major problem Spencer would like to solve, it would be the homeless crisis. As a writer for Locomotive Ventures LLC, keep your eyes open for Spencer's other books and his Entreprenerdz website sharing his experiences on topics such as: Entrepreneurship, Investing in the Stock Market, Owning Commercial Real Estate, First Time Construction Management, and his quest to help people find the most financially rewarding investment so that they can become financially free. Start Following Spencer on his quest today. Spencer would love it if you follow him at:

www.thespencerpierson.com

Facebook:

Spencer Pierson

@thetruthabouttrump

fb.me/thetruthabouttrump

Instagram:

@the_truth_about_trump_

@spence.sp

Made in the USA
Monee, IL
20 August 2026

60814929R00046